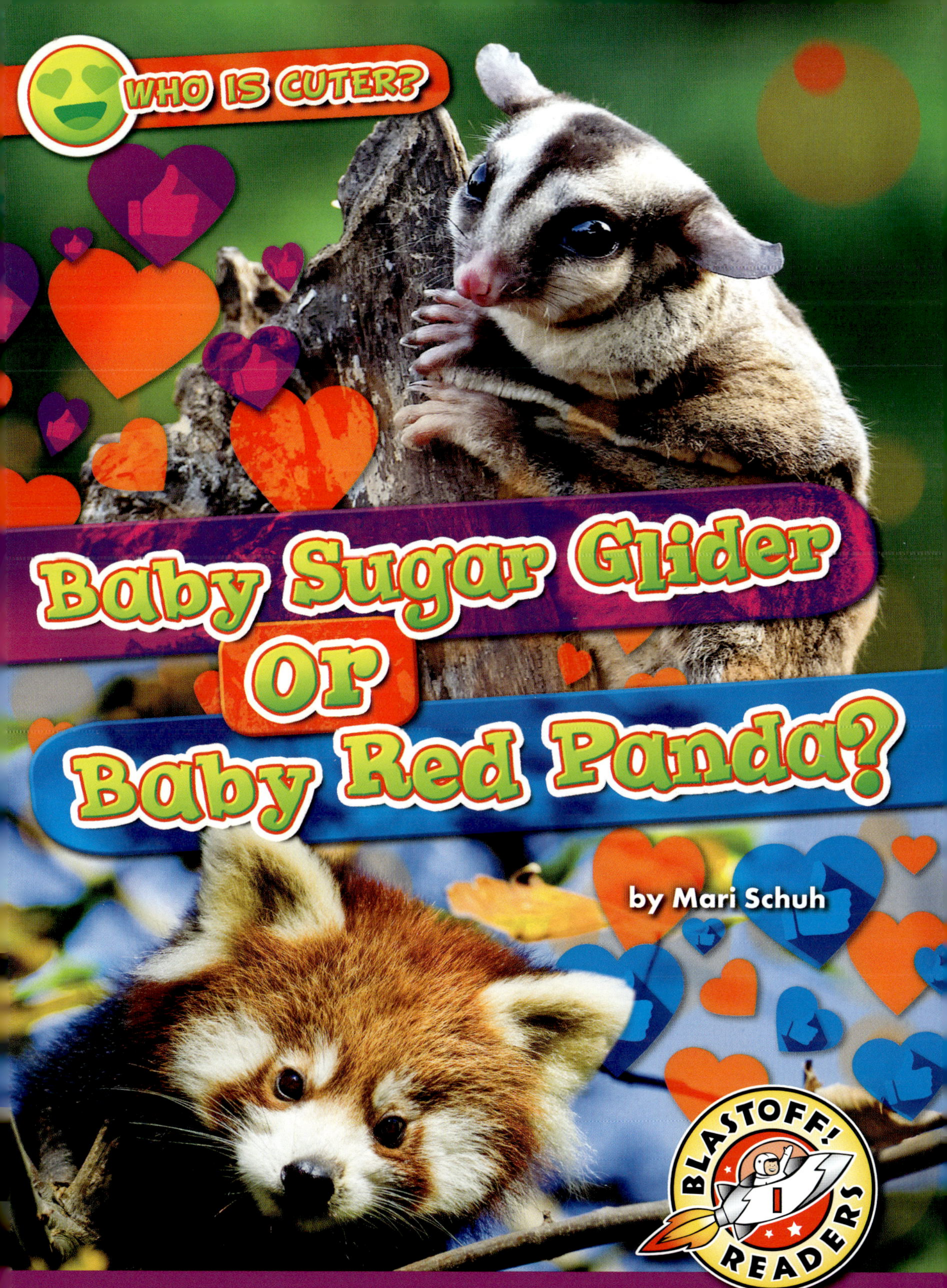

BLASTOFF! READERS, AN IMPRINT OF BELLWETHER MEDIA BY FLUTTERBEE

Blastoff! Readers are carefully developed by literacy experts to build reading stamina and move students toward fluency by combining standards-based content with developmentally appropriate text.

Level 1 provides the most support through repetition of high-frequency words, light text, predictable sentence patterns, and strong visual support.

Level 2 offers early readers a bit more challenge through varied sentences, increased text load, and text-supportive special features.

Level 3 advances early-fluent readers toward fluency through increased text load, less reliance on photos, advancing concepts, longer sentences, and more complex special features.

★ **Blastoff! Universe**

Reading Level

Blastoff! Beginners — Grade K

Blastoff! Readers — Grades 1–3

Blastoff! Discovery — Grade 4

This edition first published in 2027 by Bellwether Media, Inc.

For information regarding permission, write to Bellwether Media, Inc., Attention: Permissions Department, 3500 American Blvd W, Suite 150, Bloomington, MN 55431.

Library of Congress Cataloging-in-Publication Data is available at www.loc.gov or upon request from the publisher.

ISBN: 9798898800260 (hardcover)
ISBN: 9798898801502 (ebook)

Editor: Rachael Barnes Designer: Jennifer Bowyer

Printed in the United States of America, North Mankato, MN.

Table of Contents

Cubs and Joeys!

Baby red pandas
are called cubs.
Baby sugar gliders
are called joeys.
Both babies are cute!

joeys
cubs

These **newborn** babies are very small. Both grow soft fur. They grow long tails too.

newborn
joey
newborn
cub

Fur and Flaps

Joeys have small heads and big eyes. Older cubs have big heads. Their eyes are small.

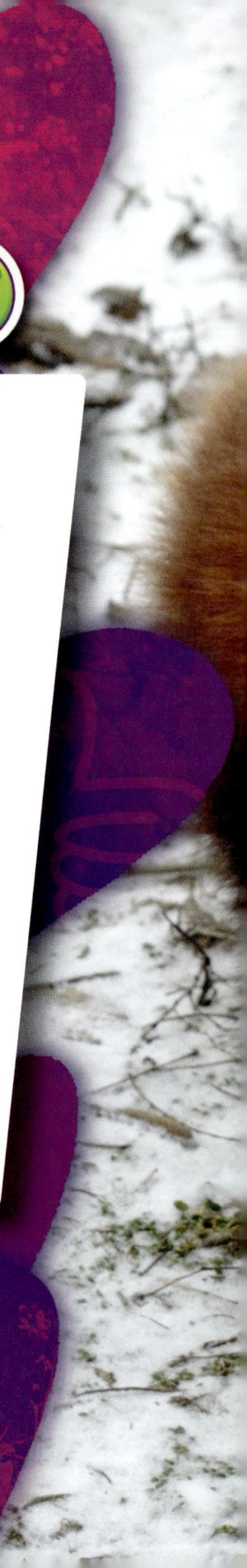

big eye

Joeys have two **flaps**.
Flaps let them **glide**.
Cubs have **coarse** fur.
They stay warm.

gliding
flap
coarse
fur

Both babies grow.
Joeys stay small.
Cubs get a lot bigger!

mom and
joey
mom
cub

Play and Rest

Cubs live in **dens**. Joeys grow in mom's pouch. Then joeys stay safe in nests.

den
pouch

Both babies learn by playing. Cubs **pounce**. Joeys chase and glide.

pouncing

Joeys snuggle.
Cubs curl up.
Which baby
is cuter?

Who Is Cuter?

Baby Sugar Glider

Who is your pick?
Vote at
BellwetherMedia.com

Baby Red Panda

lives in a den

pounces

curls up

Glossary

coarse

rough

dens

safe homes

flaps

pieces of thin skin between a sugar glider's wrists and ankles

glide

to move smoothly through the air

newborn

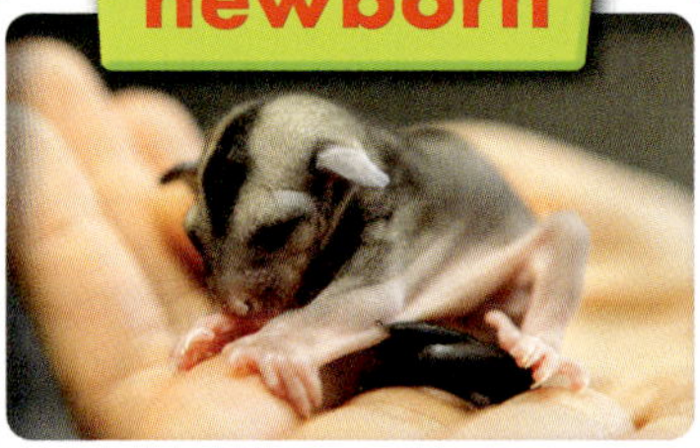

just born

pounce

to suddenly jump on something

To Learn More

AT THE LIBRARY

Bolte, Mari. *Sugar Gliders.* Mankato, Minn.: Creative Education and Creative Paperbacks, 2026.

Bowman, Chris. *Red Pandas.* Minneapolis, Minn.: Bellwether Media, 2026.

Rajczak Nelson, Kristen. *Red Pandas.* Buffalo, N.Y.: Gareth Stevens Publishing, 2026.

ON THE WEB

FACTSURFER

Factsurfer.com gives you a safe, fun way to find more information.

1. Go to www.factsurfer.com.
2. Enter "baby sugar glider or baby red panda" into the search box and click 🔍.
3. Select your book cover to see a list of related content.

Index

The images in this book are reproduced through the courtesy of: DSlight_photography, front cover (sugar glider); bertys30, front cover (red panda); Jonathan Hewitt/ Alamy, pp. 3 (sugar glider), 4-5; Praisaeng, p. 3 (red panda); I Wayan Sumatika, pp. 5, 10-11, 13, 14-15, 17, 20 (lives in mom's pouch, glides), 22 (glide); Suzi Eszterhas/ Minden Pictures, pp. 6-7, 22 (newborn); Axel Gebauer/ Minden Pictures, pp. 7, 15, 21 (lives in a den), 22 (dens); Blanka Berankova, pp. 8-9; Henrry P, p. 9; kata716, pp. 11, 22 (coarse); esdeem, pp. 12-13; Judit Dombovari, pp. 16-17, 21 (pounces); Photons_in_action, pp. 18-19, 20 (snuggles); Pascale Gueret, pp. 19, 21 (curls up); Prawalapat Nambooppha, p. 20 (sugar glider); Life on white/ Alamy, p. 21 (red panda); Aliza Thailand, p. 22 (flaps); JoshZed, p.22 (pounce).